CH

2
CHANGE

The word of God is not chained

MY SON'S STORY
GIVE LIGHT TO HIS EYES

"that the God of our Lord Jesus Christ, the Father of glory, may give to you the spirit of wisdom and revelation in the knowledge of Him, the eyes of your understanding being enlightened; that you may know what is the hope of His calling, what are the riches of the glory of His inheritance in the saints,"
Ephesians 1:17-18 NKJ

CLAUDIA BOLDEN HARDEN
A MOTHER AND SON COLLABORATION

First Edition

PAGE PUBLISHING, INC.
New York, NY

First originally published by Page Publishing, Inc. 2015

ISBN 978-1-68139-030-7 (pbk)
ISBN 978-1-68139-031-4 (digital)

Printed in the United States of America

I want to dedicate this book to prisoners
and mistreated people everywhere, the bible says,
"Remember those in prison as if you were their fellow prisoners, and
those who are mistreated as if you yourselves were suffering.

"There is no greater agony than a story left untold."
– Maya Angelou

It takes moral courage to be who you are. It's been a long ride in a dark place, but I am confessing, yes I was a victim, yes, I did victimize others and writing this book has given me the Courage to release me from me.

Like anybody else, I wish that I could have taken a different route, but being on lock down, I've had the time to experience shame, regrets, pain, sleepless nights, heartbreak, physical disconnections, near death experiences and a spiritual transition.

My life in prison is not a mistake, I actually begged God to save me from myself and He led me here to do what I asked him to do. I ask forgiveness from God and my victims, as I forgive myself and I am now able to tell the truth and share my story.

Only those who see the invisible can do the God possible.

1 Peter 5:10
And after you have suffered for a little while, the God of all grace, who called you to His eternal glory in Christ, will Himself perfect, confirm, strengthen and establish you.

Contents

Section 1

My Family

My name is Cedric Harden. I was born in 1990 on October 26. Son of Claudia Mae Bolden and Cedric Zenera Harden Sr. I grew up in Cleveland, Ohio, where the story of my life begins. My mother graduated from Shaw High School in East Cleveland. My father graduated from Job Corps, and went on to serve in the United States Army. My mother attained a bachelor's, master's, and education specialist's degrees from Kent State University. She became a teacher, counselor, and principal. My father earned associate's degree in engineering, but chose to work for the post office during the early years of my life. In 1992, my little sister Chanequa LaNae Harden was born, who happens to be my only sibling. My mother's mother (my grandma) passed away when I was six years old. My father's mom passed away before I was born. I don't remember much about any of my grandparents other than my mom's mom. She used to give me a dollar for every time I sat next to her in Sunday Services, so I always sat next to her. I do remember she was a great cook and a mother of thirteen and grandmother of many, many more.

Section 2

Cleveland Schools... Survival Mode

As a toddler, my parents were at work during the day, so my sister and me went to daycare. The name of our daycare was Shells.

I continued to attend Shell's until my graduation at the age of four. Yes, four. I started attending kindergarten at the young age of four. I attended Cleveland public schools from K-3. There were a mixture of unruly children, parents who were just barely out of their teens and teachers in a survival mode. Not to mention classrooms that exceeded forty students. Had I not been able to go home, it could have easily been considered a prison. In my elementary years, my father, mother, sister, and I lived in a condo just inside the inner city. We owned a BMW and a GMC. So for the early part of my life, I guess it would be fair to say that compared to my peers, I was pretty well off. My mother and father were usually still at work when we got out of school. So my sister and I stayed at a lady named Missy's house until one of them came home.

My grandmother passed away. I cried a lot. My sister, not too much. I was only six. Added to this tragedy was the fact that a year later, my parents divorced. The only talk I was given of the situation was the "Mommy and Daddy are going separate ways" talk. My father left. My mother, my sister, and I stayed in the condo until 1999. My father who started remodeling an apartment building in

1992 had nearly completed the building and renovation of it by this time and moved into it.

My parents are a major part of the reason I am who I am today. They are 100 percent responsible for every program I was a part of from 1990–1998. I would say that they laid the foundation. I was involved in basketball, football, baseball, soccer, roller skating. Ice skating, singing, dancing, and at least five different martial arts. I played the piano and I sang with the Singing Angels. Piano was always hard for me since I didn't like to practice. Eventually, I became pretty good at it.

My father was verbally abusive. It seemed like he changed for the worse after he and my mother divorced. He beat me and my sister with belts and extension cords. Sometimes he would beat us for no reason at all. We would spill juice or do something clumsy that a kid would do, and that would warrant a whooping from him. A man with deep-seeded issues.

My mother had a large family. Five brothers and four sisters. This means I had many cousins. Some of my cousins had kids older than me. Well, my mother did have my sister and I at the age of thirty-five and thirty-six.

Section 3

Kent Schools...Culture Shock

My mom decided she wanted to attain her master's in education. In 1999, we moved to Kent. A new journey awaited. A new life. A new beginning. A new experience. The best time in my life.

Life in Kent was much different than life in Cleveland. For one, I didn't live with both of my parents. We did not have the money we were used to have. We did have a car although I don't remember what kind it was. My mother had no job considering she was back to being a full-time student. But somehow she packed our lunches every day and kept us clothed and fed for the three years we lived there.

Kent city schools were completely one-hundred eighty compared to what I was used to. I came to Kent in fourth grade at the age of eight. I had never seen a white teacher, let alone a white student. I had *culture shock.* Where I had come from there was literally not one white person in the school building. The thought of me going to school with whites was intimidating and unusual even surreal. In Holden elementary, the school I attended it was about 80 percent white, 20 percent black. So not only did I go from a school with no whites to some whites, I came from an all-black school to an almost all-white school. A cataclysmic change. One that happened too quickly to understand its fullness.

When we first moved to Kent, we lived in a nice apartment complex with a pool and basketball court. I had a newfound love for basketball, and played every single day (after I had done my homework, of course). I played for a predominantly white recreation league that was directly across from my elementary school. I was the best in the league doing things that no one at my age could do. Of course, some were jealous and sometimes it showed, but never anything too bad. One time, we won a critical game on the account of my game winning shot. Usually after every game, the team won; we, as a team, would agree to go to Dairy Queen to celebrate. That day, the team said nothing to me and my family about going. So my mother, sister, and I went anyway. Guess who we see? The entire team and their families. One of the true examples of racisms I've experienced in my life.

In our apartment complex, I became friends with a young boy named Ahmed from Turkey. He and his family were very nice people. Ahmed always looked up to me and we would play basketball together. I used to come over to his house all the time and his parents would feed me. They taught me that if a baby has hiccups that lemon juice will stop them immediately. One time, we were with Ahmed and his mother, and my sister and I had our pet gardener snake. We found a penny-sized toad and put it in the cage with the snake. Thirty seconds later, we looked back in the cage, and the toad was halfway down the snake's mouth. Ahmed's mother tried to pull it out, but the toad was gone. The snake died two days later. I believe it was because it ingested the toad legs first instead of the head first.

In Kent, I had the chance to experiment with a bunch of different instruments like the cello, piano, saxophone, guitar, and recorder. I was decent at all of them, but the best at piano considering I grew up playing it. I had a few piano recitals in Kent.

I was also a part of the Boy Scouts of America. Another completely white organization. I was the only black person in the entire program. I met a good friend named Bogan in the scouts. We used to play Pokémon cards together. I also had my rival, Lew. Lew was the smartest fifth grader I knew at the time. We called him Webster because he knew the definition of every word I could think of. He was also in the scouts.

School was so fun. In fifth grade, my teacher used to buy us doughnuts and orange juice once a week, and at least twice a month, we would play a kickball game. Something we never got to do in the Cleveland public schools.

In the sixth grade, I attended Stanton Elementary in Kent. This experience was unimaginable. Now, I was not only in school with whites, I was in school with Korean, Chinese, Middle Easterners, Indians (from India). And many more races of people. Actually, in my homeroom, I had a foreign exchange student from Cuba who only knew how to understand English, but not speak it. Something I can't understand or explain to this day. Stanton was so fun. When I attended Stanton, my mother had moved to a smaller, cheaper apartment complex.

Section 4

Summer Obstacles and Pit Stops

Summer camp was also fun. My sister and I learned to play Chinese dodge ball and a bunch of other games. We went on field trips to water parks. We had races. A guy named Zandell who was either sixteen or the biggest twelve-year-old I've met used to bully on me, but the Bible says you sew what you reap and he ended up getting beat up by a young guy named Blake at the camp.

Cameron, my cousin, used to come down to Kent all the time with me. I forgot to mention that during my sixth grade year, my mom had attained her educational specialist degree as a guidance counselor and became the counselor at Maple Heights Middle School where Cameron attended. Cameron and I talked on the phone every day. He came down to Kent all the time. He was my best friend. We possessed the definition of true, unadulterated, friendship, and love. In sixth grade, in our new apartment complex, I met a Russian guy named Serge. How *clee-shay*. We were good friends. He invited me to dinner a lot but they were always eating something I thought was not supposed to be eaten like cow-heart. I also met a girl named Lisa, who, to only be thirteen, was a little fast for her age. Serge and I would play strip poker with Lisa and a girl named Reny. Reny was in eighth grade. These girls were fully developed at ages twelve and thirteen. We played strip poker every day inside of our tent. Something I'm sure most kids our age were not doing.

I enjoyed seeing breasts and the naked female body. At such a young age, I had a need for sex and sexual stimulation, but I just took it to be puberty. When I learned about puberty, I wanted more pubic hair. On my genitals, under my arms, and on my face. I would look in the mirror every day to see how much hair had grown.

A girl named Essa from the Ukraine used to come over to our apartment to hang with me and my sis. I had an extreme attraction to her, and her to me. She wanted to be my girlfriend but all I wanted was to touch her. Every time she used to come over, she loved to be around me. We would wrestle and roll around on the bed. Somehow, I would get an erection that would be so hard it would hurt for almost an hour after. One day, Essa and her mother came to my house with the police. Essa's mom said that Essa had told her she was raped by me. I didn't think I raped her. Had she thought so? I never forced myself upon her. I never penetrated her. I had never even seen her outside of her clothes. When the police asked Essa what happened, she said she had made the whole thing up. We did not talk again.

I was a nerd in sixth grade with no school friends. I was only ten years old in the sixth grade. I had worn glasses since I was six years old and heard every joke there was. I was a loner. However, since I was good at some sports, I was accepted. I had never had a girlfriend, and was shy about having one. My lack of female companionship mixed with my intense sexual desire led me to have an attraction to my sister. Sometimes, I would have an urge to rub on her and against her. I would know that it was not right, but it was as if an evil spirit had come inside of me and took me over. I only did it once in Kent, and my sister told on me. My mom told me it was not right and I had already known that, but it was not me who did it, but sin within me.

After my sixth grade year, I was given three crushing blows. The first crushing blow was that my mom thought I was old enough to know the truth behind her divorce with my father. We were riding in the car one day and apparently she had told my sister the news first. She asked my sister if she wanted to tell me and she said no. It was then my mom told me something I could never forget, never understand, and for a long time come to grips with. "Your father is bisexual," she said. As a young boy, this news was perplexing.

It changed everything I felt about him. It changed everything I thought I knew. It changed my perception of life itself. It was as if I could never truly trust anyone again. It changed my perception of loyalty, morality, and understanding. But that wasn't the weird part. The weird part was that all of these feelings were dwelling in my subconscious mind. Consciously, I defended him with questions like "How do you know? What proof do you have? I never even noticed, but was I supposed too?"

The second crushing blow was that my mom believed that a family member molested me when I was younger. I had no recollection of anyone doing anything to me. I had dreams that this man would be rolling over on me naked and was told by my mother that I could have perceived them as dreams because I did not want to accept them as reality. I began to think of the desire I had for girls and didn't understand how a man could possibly feel that way toward a man. The Bible says, "For we wrestle not with flesh, and blood, but the evil spirits and rules of darkness." I truly believe that only a demonic spirit or a generational curse can cause a person to be bisexual. The last and final blow was that we were moving out of Kent and to Cleveland Heights at the end of my sixth grade year. I cried for hours and begged my mother to let us stay. I wanted to stay so bad that I didn't care if someone other than my mom had to take care of me. I was not ready, and I would never be. My sister cried along with me, but of course, to no avail. We didn't pay any bills, so we did not have any percentage of the decision. I asked myself. "Why are we moving?" Kent was the best thing that ever happened to me, to us. Why would my mother want to take away the integrated and top-of-the-line school system. A chance to see my first middle school basketball game in a town where I was at my best. A safe environment. Honor roll. It did not make much sense, but I later learned my mom couldn't get a job in Kent. However, the decision was not mine and during the summer of 2002, we were back in Cleveland Heights. I had left all of my friends, the kickball games, basketball games, baseball games, and my freedom.

Section 5

Cleveland Heights...Back to Reality Middle School...Reality Check

The day we moved back to Cleveland Heights I was nervous, scared, and a little anxious. I was scared of returning to all black schools and all black neighborhoods. The black people I had been around for the last three years were..."white." And the majority of people were white. Suddenly, I felt afraid of my own race. I had experienced Cleveland before up until the age of eight, but I was about to be twelve years old. I had never been a nine, ten, eleven-year-old in Cleveland Heights. What did I need to know? What codes did I need to live by? All I knew was that Cleveland Heights would be different. We moved to Cleveland Heights/East Cleveland School district in a fairly rough neighborhood especially for a young boy coming from Kent. The first day we got there, my mother bought me a brand new bike. It was a black, silver, and green mongoose with front and back "Phat" pegs. Pretty much a top of the line bike and a twelve-year-old dream. A week and a half into the move when we had come close to finishing unpacking, and I figured I'd take my Bike for a ride. I didn't ride because I didn't want to get lost. I've always had a terrible sense of direction. I didn't even get one hundred feet away from my house when two guys came my way on their bikes.

One was tall and the other short. Both were black. The tall one yelled out, "Come off of that bike, Nigga." I rolled away in circles as not to look like I was trying to get away, but to let them know I didn't want to be any trouble. Once again, the short one shouted, "Let me take that for a ride!" I knew that if I did, I would never get it back. My mom had paid $160.00 for this bike. That was a lot of money then for a young kid to spend on a bike. I couldn't just give the bike away, but I couldn't beat both of them. I fought a good amount of times in Kent. In fact, I only lost once out of probably six fights. But I had never fought two people, and I had a feeling that if this came to confrontation, I would not get a fair fight. "I can't do that," I said soft but stern. I rolled away with my house in sight. Fast enough to speed up if need be, but slow enough to show no fear although I was shaking uncontrollably. I turned around, and they were not chasing me. "Thank God," I said. I didn't come back outside until school started and didn't ride my bike again for about four months. No one had ever tried to steal my bike in Kent. I would leave my bike outside for weeks and never even think that someone would take it. This was a whole new world to me. One, I had to adjust too fast.

*The first school I attended was a Lutheran school that was K-8. There were only about 300 kids in all at the school. We had to wear a dress code. Khakis and a white or blue polo shirt. I had not worn a dress code since I went to Cleveland schools, and had forgotten it had even existed. In Kent, there was no dress code on any level of schooling, and there was no need because the schools were amazing, but I soon learned that the dress code in Cleveland was a way to cover up the real problems. The Lutheran school I attended in seventh grade was extremely boring compared to what I was used to. I had a combination of two teachers who taught three subjects a piece and a Physical Education teacher. We even had a gym uniform. This was insane. I now know that my mother was only shielding me from the turmoil of East Cleveland city schools. Coming to Cleveland schools, I was a bit of an outcast. I was a geeky kid with glasses with no clue what style even meant. Sometimes, kids would ask what type of shoes I had on and sometimes, they were so off-brand that I had to look at the tag to know the name of them. This was another huge difference between Cleveland and Kent.

When I was in Kent, it didn't matter what brand it was. I would get shoes from Payless, clothes from Walmart, coats from yard sales, and it made no difference because the focus was on becoming a better person inside and smart made you cool. Sadly, it was the complete opposite in Cleveland. Even Cameron, my best friend and cousin, would ask me, "What are you wearing?" and I would say "clothes." "What do you mean?" Cameron got me hip to a show called IOG and Paths on BET. A show that showed hip-hop videos. One day in our basement, I was watching a video by "Nelly" called Air Force Ones. It was a song about a shoe called Air Force Ones made by Nike. I knew I had to get a pair of these and my birthday was around the corner. About a week after, I saw the video, literally everyone in my grade seven had a pair of "Air Forces." The following week, my sister and I convinced my mother to buy us a pair. Finally, I was getting a pair of Air Force Ones and made sure to get a pair I didn't see anyone else with. So I got a pair of Grey and white ones with a blue Nike sign, and my sister got some white ones with the orange bottom and outline. When I got to school, people complimented and said "wow, I haven't seen those yet." I felt really good about myself I was finally fitting in.

A guy named Brian didn't like the attention I was getting and started a fight with me in the boy's locker room. He threw a punch, missed, grabbed me, and we ended up tussling. He put his arm around my neck and I bit him as hard as I possibly could. He got up screaming and ran out of the locker room. Some people gave me a high five, others thought it was "soft" of me to bite him. After this altercation, my Air Force Ones weren't enough to keep me popular. I had no friends and my grades were beginning to reflect my depression. About six months into the school year, I begged my mother to leave. I begged to go back to Kent. It was so much better for me, for us, for our future. One thing for sure, I was done with this school. We spent a couple weeks trying to find me a new school and we ended up finding a school called Imani. This school showed me what was really going on in Cleveland schools. This school was out of control and to this very day, I could not tell you a thing I learned there that had to do with the curriculum. But I learned a few extracurricular things. In school, when the teacher would leave the room, two guys would do something called slap boxing. It was basically fighting with an open-hand instead of a closed fist. never experienced or seen anything like it. The notion of fightin fun was unheard of to me. How could someone slap me in my and I not hate them for a long time. Of course one day, my number was up and I learned quickly that it was better to lose than to not fight at all. I squared up with a guy who was around the same size and build as me. When I look back, I think we were both afraid. He was probably a little less afraid because I wore glasses and had to take them off to slap box. Surprisingly I won. I slapped him three times. I got slapped none. I didn't know how I could move that fast and had underestimated myself. After that, I slap boxed at least once a week, always beating my opponent. I remembered my younger days studying all of the martial arts. I did and realizing that I did have some fighting background. Not to mention the seven or eight fights I got into in Kent. I had fought all my life, and won most of them too.

I also learned what New York was like. I had been before but I was only three years old. This time I was twelve. New York was great. An extremely fast-paced environment. It was a great trip. We visited a school, parks, played ball, saw the Twin Tower site, bought souvenirs, and at times just relaxed. It was the best school trip I had ever been on.

Although I was good at slap boxing, I was still a bit of a loner. I had no real friends in school. I had pretty low self-esteem. I wore glasses and looked like Erkel. However, I was a handsome young man. In the middle of my seventh grade year, I begged my mom for contact lenses so that I could *lose* the glasses. She agreed to get me some and the moment I got them, I felt like a new man.

I finished off the year at Imani and finally it was the summer. I really didn't know anyone around my neighborhood so my goal was to get to know as many people as I could. Of course my best friend and cousin Cameron came over to visit all the time, and we ventured around the neighborhood. It was better to be with someone walking around than by myself especially if you were new to "the hood."

First off, I met my neighbors. I caught them outside playing baseball and they let me play. A lady named Kris and a man named Clyde with their two kids, Anthony and Clyde Jr. lived next door to us. Anthony and Clyde became my good friends. Me and my sister would stay over at their house all the time. Kris loved watching us. She did at times for no charge. Kris used to make this Mexican Cornbread that was so good I even think about it today. They also had dog named Scooby. A boxer who was very energetic and always would scare the hell out of people when I walked him around the hood. Kris had a younger brother named Meeko that stayed around the corner. I came to find out he was the leader of the hilltop gang that roamed this neighborhood. He took a liking to me.

Some kids want to fit in, but I always had an attitude that shifted more toward competiveness. I never wanted to fit in with a crowd, but rather have the crowd fit in with me. I didn't want to be cool, I wanted to define me.

I would have to say that my most outrageous memory of my eighth grade year at Imani was probably a bully named Mark. He was one of the only people tougher than me in my grade. He was a bit of a bully and literally went out with every pretty girl in the school besides maybe one or two. I believe he also had sex with most of them. He was an amazing basketball player and tried out for the team along with me and a few other guys at the school. Since the school was a charter school and inside of a building that used to have a different middle school, the previous middle school still had their team at our school. Kids from all over came to play for the team which traveled all around to play other teams. It was a great team. Mark was the best though. When the time came for final cuts, Mark did not make the team. The next day at practice, the coach told us that Mark was too old to play for the team. "How old is he?" asked one of the players. "Eighteen," the coach said. I was taken aback. "Eighteen in the eighth grade?" I said in a whisper. How was this possible? Better yet, how was this legal? Although I had many questions, even more were answered by this shocking piece of knowledge that with thought was very easy to believe. I was wondering why this guy was so strong. He had the girls, and was so good at basketball. He was an adult! The saddest part of it all was that when the school year ended, he didn't even pass the eighth grade.

I had no girlfriend that entire year at Imani. There were a lot of girls that liked me that year, and a few I occasionally gave hugs too, but I didn't have a relationship with any due to what I believe had to have been Mark scoring them all.

Imani was as violent as you would expect for any Cleveland Middle school. Kids cursing at teachers, a few fights a month, and the occasional parent beating their kids in the middle of class.

Imani had some fun teachers. We had Mr. Manny. A Jamaican man around fifty with a strong accent and hair down to his feet which he kept in a big hat. He was a Jamaican rap artist as well and although I never knew quite what he was saying it always sounded nice.

We had Mr. Swak our PE teacher who used to bring his PS2 to school and play "Fight Night" and "Madden" with everybody.

My favorite teacher I had was Mr. Luan, an African man from Senegal who was our French teacher. Mr. Luan had a brother who was a singer and lived with him. Mr. Luan owned two clothing stores and drove a Lexus. He was well off and to this day, I have no idea why he ever worked at Imani. He had a beautiful wife and had pictures with presidents and other really famous people. He was a male role model for me.

Sometimes, I look back and think to myself, was this guy in the C.I.A. or something? He introduced me to African cuisine and we would all (me, him, his brother) eat out of the same big bowl.

The school year was over pretty quick and I was just as quick roaming around the neighborhood.

Section 6

Thriving

One day, my mother called my sister and I into the living room and told us that she had received a $6,000.00 check from back child support that my father owed. During the time we were in Kent, my father was ordered to pay child support but never did. Consequently, they went into his bank account and took a large chunk of it out and paid it to my mother. My mother asked us what we wanted to do with it and my sister replied, "Let's go to California." I laughed at this notion of going to California but little did I know we would be on a plane the next few days. My sister was extremely computer savvy at a young age in within an hour got us a seven-day, six-night stay in the Anaheim Hotel in Anaheim, California, a Crown Victoria for the entire stay. Four-day passes to Disneyland and two-way tickets for all of us for a little under $2,000.

I was very excited about the trip. The last time I had been on a plane, I was only three years old. I was a little afraid about crashing. I guess when it comes to planes, that is the only thing you can really be afraid of.

As I was thinking about what California would be like, my sister tapped me and said, "Hey you better start packing, our flight leaves at six in the morning." This was insane. I then realized that when you have money, anything is possible. We just made a spur of the moment decision to take a vacation to a place none of us had ever been to, and it was all about to happen in a matter of days. I packed up all my best clothes, best shoes, and did not sleep at all. Why sleep? It was eleven when I had finished and my mother told me I would have to wake up at four to get to the airport on time. I was so excited. California! I had only seen it on TV. This is where all the stars were. I was ready to go see this place I had only heard of.

We reached the airport on time and we were "off." Walking through the airport, my sister saw India Arie. My mother didn't believe it was her, so my sister chased her down and got a picture with her. We couldn't believe it. I guess in California, you see stars all the time. When we got on the plane and saw the Jamaican artist "Beanie Man," he was asleep, and I yelled out "Beanie Man!" His bodyguard whispered, "Yes, it's him, but he's asleep." I apologized and went to my seat. I drank a lot of apple juice and orange juice because I was able to get as much as I wanted on the plane.

We arrived at the airport, headed to pick up our luggage and rental car, and drove to our hotel. California was amazing. We visited the *Ripley's believe it or not* museum, where I got to see the world's tallest man, shortest man, longest hair, biggest hand, and a bunch of other creepy and interesting things.

Wes spent a lot of time at Disneyland which was incredible. We visited a famous church. We went to Knott's Berry Farm which was kind of like Geauga Lake, but better because it was in California. We went to Hollywood Blvd. and saw the names on the stars. I got to see the Iconic "Hollywood sign." We even got to drive through the infamous Crenshaw Blvd., California, was one of the best times of my life and for that short week, I did not have a care in the world.

When we returned home and back to reality, the answering machine was filled with messages from my father cursing at my mother about not giving his money back. To no avail of course, considering we had spent half of it on a luxurious trip to California.

During the summer of my eighth grade school year, my mother was participating in a course to become a principal at Shaw High School in East Cleveland. She ended up receiving the job and by God's grace, we lived right down the street from the high school. Since my sister and I had trouble getting along and my dad wanted to cease child support payments, my parents made an agreement that I would live over at my father's house, and he wouldn't have to pay child support. I dreaded the thought of living with my father. My only memory of him was the bad ones because they were so bad. After days of begging and pleading to stay with my mother, I was defeated because I didn't respect her rules. I would be going to stay with my father for the last month and a half of the summer and the next school year. Staying with my father was even worse than I thought it would be, and I thought it would be horrible. I was made to do an abundance of chores that included vacuuming the entire apartment, cleaning the kitchen, bathroom, and washing and ironing my own clothes. I had never done any of these things at my mother's house and to me they were all punishments. I was given a measly ten dollars a week to basically be a housekeeper. Today when I look back, I am thankful for having done these chores because they gave me a sense of responsibility and character. However, my father didn't ask me to do these things to build responsibility or character, but because he was lazy. Every time I would come to visit him before I lived with him, his house was a mess. A pig sty. He didn't lead by example, he verbally abused me and I verbally abused him too. He always threatened to call the police on me. At times I would go a day without eating and most days, I would have to hear him call my mother every name in the book. This made me think it was all right to call women names like bitches and sadly my mother was included too.

Section 7

Struggles...Shaw High School

That summer was a fun summer, but soon, it would be over. My parents decided that I would attend Shaw High School in East Cleveland which happened to be the same building my mother attended as a teenager, and the school she would also become the principal. The school was split up into four small schools. I chose to be a part of the arts school, which gave me a chance to participate in programs such as choir and drama. My mother was the principal in the science and technology school.

At first I dreaded the fact that I attended the same exact school my mother worked at, but then I realized that I might get a bit of favoritism.

I was walking up to the doors, I noticed there was a line to get into the school. I stood in it and as I got closer to the door, I noticed that up ahead were metal detectors.

"Wow!" I thought to myself. "Metal detectors at a school? No wonder my mother has been keeping me from going to public school were kids brining in guns and knives into school? Was this real?" I began to wonder if I would make it through the day let alone the entire school year. My slap boxing was up to par but it occurred to me that it would not be enough.

When I finally got into the school building, I heard a voice say, "Tuck your shirt in." (It was my mother) and I replied, "Yes, Ms.

Bolden." I was warned not to call her mom in school. Shaw had a dress code but not as strict as the elementary and middle schools in Greater Cleveland. We were allowed to wear white, black, and any colored blue T-shirt, and black or blue Dickies, and black jeans. The dress code was said to have been established so that no one would feel like anyone dressed better than them, but this was East Cleveland, we were all broke.

I ran into a lot of people I knew my first day at school.

My first day at school, I had on a light blue t-shirt with black Roca wear jeans on with some all-black Air Force J's. By this time, I had understood that in the world I lived in at my age, what you had on meant more than who you were on the inside. I also had my left ear pierced. For some reason, back then, if you got the right one pierced, it meant you were gay. I also wore a sterling silver basketball chain. I was considered "fresh."

There were many gangs around East Cleveland at the time, all with different names. One more outrageous than the next. There were even female gangs at Shaw High School. They were also dangerous and visually branched off of the male gangs.

I was not in a gang. Yet but I would soon find out that it was not good to be by yourself. Since there was a choir at Shaw High school, I joined it of course. I actually did not want to join it but my mother made me so I had to. The choir was led by a soft-spoken lady named Ms. Dawn. She was very nice, but sometimes got mean if the class got too out of hand. All of the girls in the choir liked me, and this was insane to deal with. I had never experienced so many girls liking me and I began to get a "Big Head" about myself. This sometimes got me in trouble.

A girl named Shena who I had about three classes with liked me a lot. She gave me her number and we would talk on the phone sometimes. She would always give me a hug when she saw me. Shena was a bit "fast" for her age. Sometimes, we would be in the back of class and she would put her hand down my pants. I had never had this happen before and sometimes I would stop her before she did. She would then say, "Let me touch it."

I was in the choir with a girl named Dee and she also liked me.

One day, as I was walking from school to a friend's house, a couple of guys walked up to me and attempted to shake my hand.

The second I put my hand out to shake their hand, I received a hard unanticipated blow to the face followed by about nine more. I was rattled and dizzy, but I had enough in me to run away, and run I did. I ran all the way to my father's house which was about a ten-minute run, and I ran all the way there non-stop. I was scared and didn't understand why this had happened to me. Did these guys mistake me for someone else? Was I just at the wrong place at the wrong time? Who were these guys? When I got home, my father asked me what happened and since I was visibly "lumped up." I told him the truth. He told my mother and of course she was on the quest for the truth.

I was told the guy's names were Duke and Bro. They were known around the hood for fighting. Duke was an eighth grader, and Bro was a freshman like me. My mother called Bro's mother and she, him, and I all had a conference in her office which ended up in his suspension for ten days and me watching my back every day for the rest of the school year.

Section 8

Gangster...Who Me?

My friends and I decided to create our own gang. Reg told me that he got me a gun. A 22. He asked me if it was my first gun, and I told him it was. He told me that since this was my first gun that he would call me Duece. I liked the name and accepted it.

We were now in a gang and it was my duty to fight for our cause for the rest of my life.

The group was now at two and we felt like we had something. Reg and I came up with the idea that we would work out, wrestle, and slap box all the time so that we would be ready as we possibly could if and when another fight occurred.

Reg got us all guns courtesy of his "gun man" that he allegedly robbed. I already had my 22, Reg had a 357 magnum, and to Skip, he gave a 25. Nobody ever knew I had a Glock.

At the end of the school year, my mother heard that I was in a gang. At this point, I was derailed, and she decided to move, she didn't know where. I said my good-byes to all of my classmates and probably got every girl's number in my freshman class as well as a few sophomores, juniors, and seniors.

The summer of 2005 was a fun-filled summer. It was the summer I met my friend Steve. My mother approved of Steve, she knew his family. I would always see Steve around the hood and everyone knew him because he had two beautiful sisters. Steve lived literally right around the corner from me. A twenty-five-second walk if I took my time. Steve and I loved walking around the hood and enjoyed riding our bikes around the hood as well. I would stay over at Steve's house all of the time. I would literally only go home to let my mother know I was alive. Steve's room was in his basement where he had his computer set up to loud speakers and we could listen to music and play PS2 all the time. We would drink beers downstairs because his father had like a million cases of all different beers. We would walk around the hood meeting girls who I had never knew existed. Steve had a way with the girls and they loved him. This made us a dynamic duo. If Steve couldn't get the girl I could, and vice-versa. We would go to sleep at one to two in the morning and wouldn't wake up until one or two in the afternoon. We would sneak out late at night and go to girl's house to do whatever. Steve had a mother and father that lived together which was unusual for most inner city kids. They were very nice to me, and I was grateful.

For a long time, Steve didn't really have any friends who were guys so I really think that his parents were happy he had friends. Steve was the reason I first tried marijuana. I always was a little timid to try it because I didn't know what being high do to you. Our first time smoking was at Six Flags. We went with Steve's cousin from California. They told me that smoking before we got on the ride would make it extra intense. So I said, "Hey, if they're going to do it, I won't be left out." It was amazing being high. I felt so "nerveless." I laughed a lot and for once in my life only thought about the present. It was almost as if when I smoked marijuana I became…myself. It was an amazing feeling that from that day forward I had to have it or at least I behaved that way.

When the summer had ended, I got news from my mother that we would be moving, out of Cleveland Heights into a more "upscale" neighborhood called Richmond Heights.

Amazingly, I didn't like the idea. I had grown accustomed to my neighborhood and I had a lot of friends around the neighborhood. Since Steve was now my best friend at the time, I was really sad I had to leave him. Surprisingly, Steve's older sister was moving to Richmond Heights as well and he let me know he would always be over there. What a coincidence.

Section 9

Starting Again...For Real

Richmond Heights was a nice neighborhood. The school system was about 60 percent white and 40 percent black which was unusual while at the same time usual. I had experienced all blacks, and mostly white, but now it was close to even as you could get.

The first day I walked into school, it felt different. First off, there was no dress code which made me feel a little more free. Secondly, I did not know anyone and everyone knew each other. Thirdly, the high school had only about three hundred people that attended as opposed to Shaw's 1400. I had got the vibe that this school was nothing like Shaw and even the complete opposite. I was so used to be a loud, violent, gang-oriented school, and now I was in a small, quiet, "soft" school. The first day of school, I got into an argument with a guy who thought he could beat me in basketball. I told him that even if he could, he could not be at me in a fight. To my surprise he said, "We'll see." What was odd about this was that I didn't know why I said it. I had not gotten into a fight my entire ninth grade year, why was I so quick to jump into one now?

Whatever the case was, I told the guy that I would meet him in PE class in the locker room. When we got to the locker room, I asked him arrogantly "Wasp, what you trying to do." I sensed fear in him and knew he did not really want any problems. I inched closer to him repeating myself. He said nothing. *Boom.* I hit him in the face with a solid right that made him lean to the side. I was so focused on him I didn't even realize that there were almost twenty other students around us. As soon as I hit him, I heard *oo's* and *aw's*. I even heard a couple girls running out of the locker room chuckling. While noticing all of this, I lost track of the guy I hit. PE finished and before I even got dressed back into my school clothes, I got called down to the office. This guy actually told on me. I didn't believe it. I told on someone before. But I never experienced someone telling on me in front of me. It was like there was no code or anything. Didn't this guy grow up hearing the unspoken rule that snitches get stitches? Apparently not because I was suspended for three days.

When I got back to school, I was referred to by some as a tough guy and others as a bully. I didn't mind being called a bully because for once, it felt good being on the other side of the bullying. I was no longer scared, but people were scared of me. The feeling was incredible and I became addicted to it fast. As usual, I got a lot of attention from girls. I also was on the football team for the first time in my high school years. I had played for a little Pop Warner team that was humble when I was younger so I had some experience. I liked football and it was something I was naturally good at, almost effortlessly. I came in as a freshman/sophomore, but remembered I skipped a grade and was the starting varsity running back. I did okay but the team at this time was terrible, and me and a few other guys were the only decent players on the team.

I enjoyed football and the late-night practices with the cheerleaders. There weren't many girls at Richmond. At least not as many as I was used to. There was one that stuck out to me though. I would see her running around the school. Different guys would chase her, and I would wish I was one of those guys. She was beautiful. A cheerleader as well.

I eventually found out that her name was Lana. One day at Powder Puff practice, I was entertaining my coaching duties and I realized that she was a part of the game. Powder Puff is basically a football game where the freshman and Sophomore girls play against each other for bragging rights. While I was sitting down and everyone else was running around chasing each other and doing everything else in the dark of night, a girl came up to me and laid down on my lap. It was very dark and so looked down and at the girl's body features and realized that this was Lana. At this point in time, I knew her name but didn't want to let her know I did because she never told me. I didn't want to appear as a stalker or nerd. So I asked, "What's your name?" Immediately we start laughing because we both thought that it was funny that she would come be on my lap and we didn't know each other's name. She chuckled and said, "Lana." I told her my name was Cedric. I didn't want to tell her my "Street Name" because there were so many people afraid of me I didn't want her to be on that list. I wanted to appear as innocent as possible. From that day forward, Lana and I were not officially together but I would go up and give her a hug every time I would see her. Eventually I summoned the courage to ask for her number and she gave it to me. I would call her all the time and she would call and text me all the time. I liked her a lot and wanted her to be with me.

I kept in touch with my homies, we were still in the gang business. We were eight strong now. Social networking was in its early stages at the time, and so we told everyone to create a Myspace and tagged page repping C.O.D. Everyone around the school began to know who we were. Some liked us. Some didn't. I got a hoodie made at the mall with "C.O.D. for life" on it, and would wear it around the school so that people knew we were serious.

In school, every girl that wasn't afraid of me loved me. I would give girls nicknames and they would take them and wouldn't answer to anything else. In light of my accomplishments, a girl named Jamie, a white girl, took a huge liking to me. She invited me over to her house the day after I met her. We watched movies for a while and eventually she turned around and kissed me. We kissed for a while and then she gave me oral sex. This was my first time ever receiving oral sex, and it was all right. I thought it would have been better, but I thought that maybe she wasn't doing it right.

Since the group was beginning to really grow, we had a party for C.O.D.

Section 10

Set Up

About the third month into the school year, Zizzy had the bright idea that we would break into C's house (our arch enemy) and steal whatever he had of value. I debated over this silly idea for a couple of weeks and decided that I would assist him as a lookout only. So one day, I came over to Zizzy's house with my gloves and mask and he was ready to do this. We walked over to C's house, which was down the street from Zizzy's house, where there were two cars parked in the driveway. Immediately, I looked at this as a sign to turn back. Zizzy, however, told me that he had been scouting this house out and that although there were two cars in the driveway, no one was home. Believe it or not, I took his word for it and we walked around to the back window. The back window was unlocked and he opened it with the assistance of me lifting him up. As he was opening the window, I saw the appearance of an adult male in the back door which was a sliding, see-through door. I dropped Zizzy and we both fell on the ground. We got up and started running as fast as we could through back yards and bushes. I was running much faster than Zizzy and reached his house before he did. He showed up five minutes later. After he got there, the police were knocking on the door. I hid in the closet and Zizzy opened the door. About a minute after, I heard him open the door. I was greeted by Richmond Heights Police with a gun pointed toward my face. I got up slow, hoping that I did not get shot.

A bunch of things did not make sense to me. For one, why did I make it back to Zizzy's house so much faster than he did? Second, how did the police know to come straight to Zizzy's house? Even if the man, who we later found out was C's father, saw our faces, how could he know who we were. He had never seen us a day in his life.

I didn't understand all these things. But what I really couldn't understand, and what really bothered me and irks me to this very day is the fact that I went to the juvenile detention center that night and Zizzy did not. I felt framed almost. It was like I was set up and I was, but I did not know by who. Could it have been Zizzy?

That night for the first time in my life I was sent to the juvenile detention center. I was afraid. I had heard about the juvenile center also known as "The Duece" from some of my peers in East Cleveland. I had never been locked up and it felt wrong. It didn't feel like a human being should be locked inside somewhere against his will. Many thoughts ran through my head while I was sitting in booking. Was I going to do "hard time?" Did Ziggysnitch on me? Would I have to move back with my father? Would I go back to Richmond?

When I got my clothes and blanket, I went to a room filled with guys who were around the same age as me. Some a little older and some a little younger. I was fourteen. There were cells inside of the room, but no one actually resided in them, instead there were cots on the ground for people to stay on. I was assigned to a cot. A lot of people asked me where I was from and I would tell them East Cleveland. They would ask if I knew people and asked if I was in a gang. I would tell them I was GD. Some were also GD, and would test me to see if I knew the knowledge of my set. I would end up teaching them things. We watched movies at night and played basketball during the day. What was shocking to me was how well I fit in. I fit in so well that it was almost scary. Did I belong here? I had thought I was better than these guys. But I was not so different. On my third day there, I went in front of a magistrate and was sentenced to three days with time served which meant I would be leaving that day. While in court, my mother told the judge that my father would be taking custody, and my heart sank. I dreaded living with him and sometimes I thought death was better. He never did anything for me. Fed me maybe twice a week, and I literally had to do everything but the bills which amounted to barely anything because he was the owner of the building he resided in.

I was told that I would now be going to Glenville High School which was down the street from where my father lived. Glenville was a school that was based around sports. They had the best football team in the state and were ranked seventh in the country. Glenville also had a beef with Shaw High School which left me in a dilemma. If I said I had come from Shaw, I could run into beef with someone. If I said I came from Richmond, people would think I was soft and I would have to fight to prove I wasn't. Reg was happy to hear the news that I was coming back to the "Hood." My father lived in a building he owned on 105th and St. Clair Ave. A very part of the inner city and widely recognized for its drugs and violence. Glenville was an all black school with a surprising amount of white teachers.

Section 11

Glenville High School

My first day of school at Glenville I didn't talk to anyone. My goal was not to get into a fight because I had none of my gang members with me. After attending Glenville for one day, I was so uncomfortable I didn't go back the next day or the day after, or the day after the day after.

I didn't want to go back so my mother and father decided I would go to an alternative school in Cleveland Heights. It was a computer-based school that had teachers that would really only assist if you didn't understand what was going on with the computer. It would start at eight o'clock in the morning and be over at twelve. I would come to school almost every morning high out of my mind. He would be gone for eight and nine days at a time. He would usually leave me around fifty to seventy-five dollars which was never enough. I would spend half of it on marijuana and the other half on fast food and at the corner convenience store which was very convenient, considering it was only about one hundred feet away from my dad's building. I would argue with my father every day and for days at a time would not speak to him. He never bought me anything while I was living with me, and our arguments were very intense. He would threaten to kill me, call the police on me, and threaten to call my probation officer. I had been put on probation for my involvement in attempting to break in C's house.

Since I finished out the year at Glenville without getting into any trouble, my mother decided after much pleading from me, that she would let me move back in with her.

The first thing I did on my trip back to Richmond Heights was to go to the mall. I called up my road dogs and the rest of the click and told them to meet me at the mall. We all met up at the mall and walked around the mall as we usually did throughout the summer.

Summer came to a close. I had finished my junior year, my probation, which had been in effect since my attempted burglary was also coming to an end. To my luck, my mother allowed me to come back to live with her in Richmond Heights, and also informed me that I would be finishing my senior year at Richmond High School. I simply wanted to finish the year off with good grades, but I would have to prove that I wasn't the same. Everyone already knew what they thought of me.

During the summer, I had moved back to Richmond with my mother to get ready for the school year. I verbally said, "I left our gang and its memories behind, but I was actually living a double life, one before my mother and another away from her, who was I?"

Section 12

Senior Year...Yes Me

Although Richmond had become more urban during my time away, it was in no way, shape or form compared to what was going on in the inner city of Cleveland. Armed with this knowledge, I realized that all the things I had once had to endure, I would no longer have too!

Although a lot of people were the same, there were different ones as well. And some of the ones who knew me still liked me because my violent ways which were foreign to them intrigued them.

That night I had a dream that the police were looking for me inside the Kamikakze and when they found me in the restroom, they shot me and I woke up.

About three months into the school year, I started to attend a church with my mother. During this time, I attained a very close relationship with God. I read my Bible every day, went to Bible study every Tuesday, praise team practice every Thursday, and church every Sunday. I was what one would call "on Fire for the Lord." I felt at home. Pastor started a group for young men where once a week we would come into the church and play video games, sometimes go to the park, and of course have a study of the word to help us become better young men. I couldn't stay away from the church during this time. I was there four days a week. Pastor and I would visit other churches to let them know about our programs and that young men and women could come to the church to stay off the streets.

One day we had a pastor appreciation day at the church, and I broke down in tears about how Pastor had helped me change my life. He responded by letting me know that I would be great for the Lord and that everything that I touched would literally turn to gold. The church became my second home. My mother decided to change churches, I begged my mother to allow me to continue attending Pastor's church. I had quit smoking, quit drinking, and even with much prayer, attended a job interview to work for UPS all at the age of seventeen. She elected that I would not be able to attend Pastor's church, and that I would follow her where she went. This bothered my heart. For once, I had a reason to do good. A reason to quit all the things that were bringing me down. But she didn't know how much I gave up! I had surely attained the Holy Spirit, but as of now I had no roots, no foundation, and my church family was completely taken away from me, I thought! Today I know the church is in you, not in a building.

With much prayer and supplication, I attained the job at UPS at the age of seventeen. I was hired with about three other people out of about 10,000 people so I very much thought it was a blessing and gift from God. I finished the school year with a 3.89 average for the year and a 3.1 for my high school career. I graduated and for my last semester received straight *A's*. Of course I asked my mother about the car I was supposed to receive in exchange for my straight *A's,* and my mother told me that she was not going to buy me one because I was not ready. I didn't understand what she meant. She must have found out about some things I tried to hide. I was seventeen, I had a good job. I hadn't stayed out late for three months and I had straight *A's* in a school that I was kicked out of two years ago. If I was going to be ready at any time, it was going to be then, but my mom lied to me and it hurt me. Now not only did she pull me out of the church, the only reason I was doing well in my life, but she also lied to me which made me draw back in my faith. I was determined to get my own car, and I eventually did.

Section 13

College It Is... Kent State University

My mother wanted me to go to school and let me know that if I didn't, I couldn't stay in her house. I did the analytical thing and decided not to be homeless. I agreed to go to school. My mother told me that this would be a good plan. My father bought me a top of the line $2,000.00 laptop computer with fingerprint login, a camera, and much more. I was very appreciative of this because it was not very often that my father did something for me. A lot of people were happy about me going to college, but my comrades and friends were upset. They felt as if I were leaving them.

It seemed as if my gang-life was finally over, and that now I just had a bunch of guys who I could call my friends. The day I moved into my dorm, JC helped me, along with my mother and sister. I gave everybody hugs good-bye. I let them know I would try to call all the time, and that they wouldn't miss me as much as they thought and then I fell asleep. I dozed off basking in the realization that I was on my own now. I could do whatever I wanted. In the middle of my sleep, I heard a knock on the door. It was a white guy and I presumed to be his mother and father. While they were coming in with his luggage, I realized I only had on my underwear. I hurried and tried to gather my clothes and compose myself. They giggled and told me that it was all right. "My name is James" said the 5'6" white guy who I now realized was my roommate. I helped him settle in and soon enough his parents were also gone. James and I arrived on campus around 10:00 AM and it took about seven to eight hours to unpack, set up, and tidy up. After we were done getting our room together, we got in the shower. “Do you want to meet a couple of people?” James asked. “Why not?” We went through the hall of our all freshman dorm knocking on doors. It was co-ed, so one whole hall was female the other male. While we were walking through the hall, I remembered that I had brought about a quarter of weed down with me. After we finished walking through the hall and meeting people, James asked me if I wanted to go to some “Frat Parties” that were supposed to be happening that night.

I had never been to a fraternity party, let alone a white one before, but I was at KSU. I was ready for a new side of life. I ended up agreeing to go and we invited a complete “stoner” named Matt who lived about two doors down and a guy named Jeff that James went to high school with. “I wish we had some Bud,” said Matt. It was then I remembered that I had some. I told the guys to give me a minute while I went to “see what I could do.” As I went through one of my bags looking for my weed, I found about a half of a blunt that I had smoked with LC on the way to KSU. Since Jordan didn’t smoke and neither did his friend this would surely suffice for Matt and I. When I walked outside, the guys were waiting. “I think I might be able to help with that one problem.” I said to Matt. He smiled and we went on our way. The frats were about a fifteen-minute walk from the freshman dorms and about midway through the walk I sparked up the half a blunt. I took a couple hard hits and passed it to Matt who took even harder hits. He smoked like a true “stoner.”

We finished the blunt with about a minute left until we reached the “Frat’s.” We stopped at the “Circle K store” and Jordan, my roommate, who happened to have a fake ID bought a case of beer I had never heard of before called Keystone light. As we were walking to the first Frat house, I realized that my “high” had kicked in, in a major way. I was so high, I forgot the names.

A couple days later, I found myself running into a couple of people I went to elementary school with from Kent. They invited me to a party in the freshman dorm that was directly across from us. I decided to go to see what it was all about. To my surprise, it was an all-black party like the ones I was used to at home. Girls "twerking" and grinding on guys and each other. Sex with clothes on as I like to think of it. I ran into a couple of Shaw High students I went to school with. They asked me did I have any weed, and since I was down to only a couple blunts, I told them that I was dry.

Dude ran through a couple instrumentals until he stopped at one that we all liked.

I instantly fell in love with the instrumental. He played it for thirty seconds before I told him to run it from the top. He said it was five minutes thirty-eight seconds. He played the instrumental and immediately I was spitting off bars that I had no idea where they came from. I didn't know where the words were coming from as I said them. I was putting together metaphors and my word play was unlike anyone I had ever heard before. I rapped for the entire beat and when I was finished, everybody in the room looked like they had no clue where they were before, and knew exactly where they were now. They were at the "Young Deuce Show." Everyone was wide-awake as if they had seen a ghost or a celebrity they had wanted to see all of their life. They touched me in awe. A guy that looked like a white version of Lil Wayne said, "I have heard a lot of good rappers and my favorite of all time is Lil Wayne, but I kid you not, that was the hottest shit I ever heard in my life." "He's better than Wayne," said another. "He's fucking amazing," said Kyle. The most ironic part of it all is that I had already known this. It was as if I was listening to something inside of me. For five minutes and thirty-eight seconds, I spit the hottest rap I had ever spit in my life, written or freestyle without pausing and without thinking what my next word would be. I knew it was better than Wayne. I knew that I or no one else had heard anything better in their life. I also had the odd and ironic certainty that I would never, as long as I lived, rap that good again. I would not even make an effort because what I did was effortless. I really wanted to take credit for it, and give the weed half and myself the other, but I couldn't. It wasn't me that spit that rap, it was a spirit. What spirit, I don't know. Good or bad, but I knew that although I could make great music if I tried, it would never be like that.

In that moment I decided that I would get back into making music and put a mix tape out. I knew all of the essentials, and that's where I wanted to take my life. The school year went on, and D and

I got closer. We went to the recreation center to work out or play basketball. Every weekend, we would find ourselves at a club I had to sneak into because I didn't turn eighteen until October of 2008. We became good friends.

The election of 2008 came, and of course, D and I were hoping Obama would win. We were at a restaurant during the election where a lot of people hung out, and during this particular occasion, we watched and waited for Obama to win. We shot pool for a while and when the news came that he had won, all that was heard was cheering and clapping, whistling, and chanting, "Yes we can!"

The news spread across campus like a virus and everybody got wind that people would be meeting up outside the towers. D and I decided to pay the towers. Since I had a twenty-dollar bill in my hand, I cashed it in for one's. When we got there, we were astonished to see the crowds of people gathered to celebrate the win of the first president of color. There were blacks, but more amazingly, there were just as many whites. Diore and I entered the crowds changing different obscenities with different people as we made our way to the center. When we found ourselves in the middle of the crowd, I told D to lift me up in the air and when he did, I pulled out my stack of one-dollar bills and threw them in the air. As they flew across the sky, everyone tried to grab as many dollars as they could. I felt good about the win and where I was from, when you felt good, you threw money. Of course you were usually majorly under the influence of something, when you did, but I was high on life.

D introduced me to some clientele and I sold my eighths for $25 dollars. I kept one and when D and I smoked a blunt of it, we weren't even high. It was almost impossible to find some good weed. It was nonexistent on campus, which baffled me because at home, that's all there was. An idea sparked in my head. D had introduced me to "Stick Man" who had sold weed. I had bought a quarter ounce and a couple of five sacks from him a few times, but nothing large. I wanted to buy two ounces. I knew all this campus needed was a guy who sold consistent good weed for regular prices. I called stick man up and asked him what he would want for two ounces. I would pay $225, which for the quality of weed he had given me in the past was a good deal.

In a matter of two weeks, I had been introduced to eight people who purchased marijuana from me. All of them were willing and ready to pay for what was obviously the best mid-grade marijuana around campus. In two months, I was the man. Grossing about $700.00 a week profit. I had more money than I could've made with any job I was able to get at the time.

As far as grades went, I maintained an average which was, for my major, not up to standards. I had a 2.3 and needed a 2.75 to stay off academic probation.

Section 14

Having Sight but Can't See

During the end of the school year, I started to skip class. I had lost twenty-five pounds from the time I started school. I would hide it from my family. All I did was smoke and drink. I felt extremely unhealthy. At times, I couldn't even breathe and would still puff away. I couldn't stop. I was a weed head and alcoholic. I finished the year by quitting a week before all of my final exams, sabotaging a chance to go the next year. I had four unpaid parking tickets. I acquired a car with my weed money. I even slapped a girl in my dance class at a rehearsal because I thought she had a smart mouth and received a disorderly conduct ticket which cost me $175.

At the end of the school year, I packed up and came home to my mother's house. My sister had dropped out of school and attained her GED. She chose to start a career as a nursing assistant where the starting pay was 12/hour. When I came home for the summer, I continued on my path of turmoil. I came home with $800.00, my car, and an ounce of weed.

During the summer, my mother got the vibe that I was not going back to school. She urged me to get a job every day and let me know that if I didn't get one, I could not stay with her. Since I didn't have a job, I would go over to my father's house and clean up the various rooms for $25–30 a piece twice a week. This gave me a chance to get closer to him and sometimes, I would even willfully spend the night for days at a time.

Since my mother was pressing me to get a job, I started going on Craigslist to find one. There were ten to fifteen new job openings every day on the site. I ended up landing a job in an upscale hotel in Aurora. I had a car I would take the forty-minute drive every day to the hotel and fold blankets and sheets for my four-hour shift. Since I worked at the hotel, I would get a lot of free food from there. The food was definitely five star. The chicken tasted better than the steak. They had a wine room that was filled with every liquor and wine I could imagine. I wanted to steal some, but never had the opportunity. After a month, they stopped calling me to work. The job was through a temporary service and they let you go whenever they wanted, if you weren't needed. After this, I attended a job interview at a dance studio. I didn't think I'd get the job as a dance instructor, but I went to the interview. The dance studio was nice, and I was the only black person at the fifteen-person interview. We practiced salsa, ballroom, and even a little hop. I exceeded everyone else because of their lack of rhythm even though I had no formal training. The job included paid training. The dancers took trips all over the world and they had pretty ladies working there.

Section 15

Dumb me...Liar

Toward the end of summer, T asked me to go to a club, but I told him that since school was about to start back that there were probably going to be parties in Kent, and that I wanted to go there and he could join me. My car was broken down. It had stopped one day down the street from my house. Since I knew nothing about cars, it was going to stay that way. My sister was doing well at her new nursing job—bought a car that she let me drive from time to time.

I called my sister that night asking and pleading for the car when she got off work at ten. Time and time she told me no, but I persisted, insisted, and I told her I let her use mine, how she wasn't being a good sister, and how she shouldn't treat her brother this way and even then she still said no. I lied down in my bed almost asleep, but I asked her one last time as she walked through the door and to my surprise she threw the keys, but what I didn't know is that this would be one of the last days I would have as a free man.

I picked up T in my sister's grey Dodge Intrepid. We passed the club Ice on the way to Kent and he said, "Man, that bitch look like it's shaking." However, my heart was set on Kent.

I drove 80 MPH to make it to Kent in under forty minutes. The school year hadn't started yet, but I called some guys at "the House" and they told me there would be a few parties on university. I bought a twelve-pack of Budweiser, so I knew we would be all right on alcohol. "The House" always had weed so I wasn't worried about that. We pulled up in the driveway which was always packed on party days. T and I made our way upstairs to Car's room. Car's girlfriend from Florida was there. I asked, "Where's the Bud?" and he said, "Preston was suppose to come over with it later." I shared a couple beers with Car and his girl before I left to find a couple parties. T and I went from house to house, even stopping at one where a girl tried to steal one of my beers. I caught her though, told her not to do it again, and because I was already drunk, gave her the beer anyways. As we walked to the infamous Robin Hood Bar / Club, I spotted Van, who used to bring liquor over to Nikk's house. We went into the Robin Hood, drank a pitcher of beer and head out, the club was next to empty. Van pulled out a knife and some brass knuckles and asked, "Do you want to fuck someone up?" I was very drunk at the time and didn't really understand what was going on, said yes. We headed toward campus on foot, spotted a couple people. The urge came over me to not harm these people, but to rob them. I had spent most of my weed money on gas and more weed, and I just caught an open container ticket that cost me $260 dollars. I needed the money. "Give me the knife," I told Van. I ran up to two guys walking around campus. "Give me everything and don't make me use this." I whispered. They pulled out a combined $300.00, and it felt good. Coming up on free money like this gave me a high that could only add to the one I was already undergoing. The spirit I felt in me wanted to feed on the helpless. It was more than just me taking money from people. I fed off their fear and from there, I continued.

Next, we spotted a guy by himself who Van approached with the brass knuckles. He had eighty dollars. We headed toward Van's apartment building where his roommates were staying. He said he had some alcohol, and we were all over it. Nearing Van's complex, we spotted a pizza man, we began to walk fast toward him. The pizza man ran to his car and sped off. He must have known what we were thinking. We went into Van's house, his roommate was watching TV. "Yeah, man, we just robbed some mother fuckers," said Van in a voice that showed he had never done anything like this before. I had been robbing people a lot during my childhood. We drank some more before we headed back out to rob some more people.

Outside, we spotted two females, I ran up on the two and pulled the knife out on them. "Hey, give me all your money," I yelled. "No, help, help," one of the girls screamed. I tugged at one of the girls' purses that she held onto for dear life before I realized that she wasn't going to let go. We darted back to the apartment. When I finally reached "the house," I hopped in my car and drove home. On the way, Van and I talked about how he had never done anything like this before, and I gave him a few bucks. I told him the next time we would go to club Ice. Unbelievably, the next morning, my mom and I drove down to Kent. She still had hope in me even though I was now going to be on academic probation unless I changed my major. We visited the admissions office which told us I had a bunch of unpaid parking tickets which she paid, and one for disconnecting my fire alarm, which was almost a felony. They said I needed to be a better student, and write an essay on why I should be able to continue attending KSU.

We left campus and visited a new apartment complex being built for students. I was now a sophomore and didn't have to live on campus. The apartments were beautiful. You could have between one and three roommates and they were brand spanking new. The apartments came with a new TV, fridge, stove, and everything else. The apartments were so beautiful and all I could think of was how many girls I could have over to party, and how cool it would be to have my own apartment. My mother made the promise that she would allow me to go back to school, but I had to get it together. I was finally ready to redeem myself. I had another chance once again.

When we got home that day, the dance studio wanted to hire me, and they asked me to come in for a second interview, but to come in dressed up. A few days later, I asked my mother to use her truck to go to the second interview. She said that would be okay if I dropped her off at her office because school was about to start back to school, and she needed to catch up on some things.

I walked into the studio. They went over the basics of the job, and I was told the job included paid training, trips around the world, and started at $14.00/ per hour. It felt like the job for me. "Me, a *dance* teacher." I thought this was amazing.

On my way home from the interview, I was pulled over by the highway patrol for speeding. I was doing 86 mph and was written the very first ticket of my driving career. I was afraid to let my mother know about this ticket I received in her car, in fear that she would never let me drive again, so I figured I would keep it from her and with the money from this paid training, I would pay for it.

When I finally got home, it was one, and I was so tired. I hopped in the recliner in my mother's room and dozed off watching the TV.

Section 16

More Lies...They Got Me

"Knock, Knock, Knock." I heard on the door! A forceful, threatening knock. As I opened the door with no shirt and a pair of beige slacks, I realized that I was now standing in front of two police officers. I opened the screen door. I opened the screen door and one of the policemen asked, "Is that your car parked across the street?" "Yeah," I answered.

Immediately, one of the policemen, who was extremely muscular, grabbed my arm with a grip so strong that I knew an attempt to try to budge would only end up in me getting hurt. "You're under arrest," said the policeman as he cuffed me up.

I had no idea why I was under arrest. This wasn't my first run in with Richmond Heights Police. In fact, it was at least my fourth time being inside the jail. I was thrown into a holding cell. I was told I could make a call or two if I needed to which I knew was the usual protocol.

I called my mother with fear and timidness. "You're going to have to have someone bring you home from school." She asked why, and I told her, "I'm in jail." I said in a voice that made her understand that this was serious, and that I probably wasn't getting out today. As I hung up, a voice yelled out, "Kent police dept. is coming to pick you up." Immediately, my heart sank and I knew what this was about. I just didn't understand how they knew.

I waited three hours in a freezing holding cell, wearing nothing but my slacks and a black T-shirt that I picked up on my way out of my house before the two officers walked me to their car. As we drove to Kent, the officer asked, “Do you know what we are picking you up for?” “No.” I answered. “Weed or something?” I said in hopes that this was all a dream. “Robbery,” he said. We stopped at a McDonald’s that was at about the halfway mark, and the officer ordered me a chicken select meal. I thanked him and ate the whole thing in about thirty seconds. When we finally got to the Kent police station, I sat in a room alone while a black police woman who looked like she was only sixteen years old accompanied me. I talked to her for a while about how she looked pretty and didn’t look like a police officer before the police man who bought the McDonald’s for me walked back in.

“You know why we are here,” he stated in a manner that said let’s get this over with. “Is this about weed or something?” I asked hoping that this wasn’t the worst. “Do you know a guy named Van?” the detective asked. “Yes, no, kind of. Van who?” I stuttered. He pulled out a picture of Van and I along with Don at the Circle K Store that night to buy some cigarettes, and I hadn’t even remembered us walking into the store that night until they showed me the pictures. “Is this you, I, the picture?” he asked. “Yeah, I believe so.” I responded and immediately regretted. “We already have, Van,” he announced as if to say quit with the shenanigans. I was questioned by the detective for hours, only admitting that I had ran into Van that night but that we had only said our hellos, good-byes, and went our separate ways. After the first detective left, about ten minutes later, a second one came in. A white guy who looked like the first one’s brother.

“Van has admitted to his part in this crime,” “Just come out with it and you may get less time.” I refused to admit anything. Questions then arose about whether I remembered certain incidents including the incident with the two girls and the pizza man. Van had told them everything, but not about Don. My information was not difficult at all to obtain considering the fact that I attended KSU and all of my information was public. But no one knew about Don. The police had even shared my picture to Nikki and asked her if it was me. For some reason that I don’t know, she told them that it was me. I guess she was nervous and didn’t want an obstruction charge. After three hours of interrogation, the two detectives, now both in the room, concluded with letting me know that I would be doing some years for this crime, and that if I wanted to do less time then I would have to tell him who the third guy ways, that being Don, and give them any information that led to him. The thought never crossed my mind to tell on Don mostly because of the Hood code, "Snitches get Stitches." But because of my own moral code that says why should we all do time. It won't make me feel any better just because all of us got locked up. "If they don't catch him on their own, he wouldn't be caught," I said to myself. After four hours, they cuffed me up and put me in the back of the cruiser with the only new information being that now I had admitted that I was in the photo with Van. We took a twenty-minute drive to the Portage County Jail where I sat in holding for another four hours freezing almost literally to death. I was stripped down to nothing by a black correctional officer and sprayed with some type of substance before I was given a box. The box had the handbook, two blankets, toothbrush, toothpaste, and nothing else. I was cuffed and escorted to a block that looked like a prison in the movies except for the fact that the cells were not made of bars. It was about 2:00 AM so no one was out. There were about fourteen cells in the block/pod. All single man cells. There was one shower in the block. Four steel tables and a TV connected to a pole that made it only visible while sitting at three of the four steel tables and the cells in the corner. I was taken to the cell upstairs, all the way in the corner. Immediately, I lay down and to my left on a desk on the table, I saw a Bible. I had been doing a lot of things to hurt myself as far as drugs were concerned, and if I had continued down that road, I was sure the outcome would have been bad for me. At that very moment, in that cell, I felt a sense of relief. Even though I knew that I would not be seeing the outside world for some time, I felt peace. A peace that surpassed all understanding. Immediately, I opened that Bible and began to read. I had to once again allow Jesus into my heart. I had to go the narrow way.

The next morning, our doors opened simultaneously. There was no officer inside of the actual pod, but two worked in the center behind two doors outside of the pod. There were four pods CMI—3CM4. I was placed in CM3. I had never been to jail before and didn't know what to expect. I had watched movies about prison and prayed that the representation of prison and jail in movies did not relate to the real thing. When the doors opened, I walked down stairs with four other people and a couple inmates from downstairs walked to the steel tables. An officer came in with breakfast trays and everyone lined up to receive one, and I joined in. When I got my breakfast tray, I was starving and all I could think of was the movie *Life* with Martin Lawrence and Eddie Murphy. The part where the really big guy tries to take Eddie Murphy's cornbread and he wouldn't give it up. I hoped no one took anything from my tray. I would have to fight and even if I lost I would not care. I sat next to a Lean Butt guy with a beard that looked like, however, long he was there, it had never been cut. A skinny white guy with a bad cut was the last to get his tray and when he did, he walked over to my table and gave the guy with the beard his food. As the skinny white guy watched, walked away the guy with the beard cleared his throat. The skinny white guy turned around. The guy with the beard motioned him to come back with two fingers as if he had wanted what was left on his tray and he did. The white guy gave him the rest of the tray and went back to his cell almost looking as if he was ready to cry. I made no eye contact with the guy with the beard in hopes that he wouldn't signal me to give him anything off of my tray. Thankfully, I finished my entire tray and since everyone else went back to their cell to sleep, I followed suit.

Later that day, I woke up to find everyone talking, playing cards, and watching TV in what was called the "day room" downstairs on the meal tables. I came down and sat at a table with another guy who looked like he was out of place. I had never felt so alone. I had no way to call home. I knew nobody. All I had to my name was the soap, toothbrush, paste, and deodorant I was given by the jail. "Hey, what's yo name, where you from?" asked the guy with the beard as he shuffled the cards. "Ced. But they call me Deuce," I responded. "I'm from Cleveland, but I caught my case in Kent." I explained my case to him. "Oh yeah, everybody knows your case. You were the one robbing those Kent State Students." "Yeah that's me." I replied with shame in my voice. The guy with the beard's name was C.C. He was a part of a robbery turned robbery/murder. He and a few of his friends tried to rob an elderly guy for his money. They ran up into his house hoping to find a safe that had heard about. "C.C." was just the driver and had no real knowledge of the robbery prior to the day. I was told by him that he had picked those guys up and dropped them off with the knowledge that they were going to rob him and get out. Bad turned to worse when they beat the old guy up and put him in the ICU only to escape with some quarters. The ironic part was C.C. and one of his codefendants, a girl got caught at a Giant Eagle trying to exchange the quarters for one dollar. The old guy died over thirty days after being in the ICU and somehow C.C. and all of his codefendants were charged with murder along with a bunch of other charges.

Later that night at 7:00 PM, I was given my "Secret Indictments." And found out that I had been charged with four counts of aggravated robbery.

The next day, after breakfast, I showed DD my indictments to which he was completely surprised. "You are facing a lot of time youngin'," he said. "Forty years," he continued. I laughed for a couple seconds just knowing he was joking around, but his face was just as straight and mean as it had been looking, and the big beard didn't help any. "Good looking out." I said in a low tone as I walked back to my cell and pushed the little button inside of it to signal the guard to close it. I began to feel sick and tried to think how big of a mistake I made. How this could happen to me was beyond belief. Me facing forty years was beyond belief. Was not yet nineteen years of age. All I could do was resort back to my bible, my only comfort at the time. Later on in the day, I've seen C.C. reading probably the biggest book I had ever seen along with another guy.

I walked downstairs, and out of curiosity asked what the book was. "This here is a law book," he said. "It got your case in it too. I'll let you see it later." I was kind of relieved, but afraid at the same time. I really wanted to see if I was facing the amount of time that DD said I was facing, but if it was time I felt I could not stomach it. Later on that night before we locked down, C.C. slid the book through the slot in the middle of the door that was used to slide our trays through if we were locked down. I looked up aggravated robbery, and found what I was being charged. I was being charged with a felony of the first degree which was the worst kind of felony you could have been charged with. It carried a minimum of three years and a maximum of twelve years putting my minimum at twelve years and my maximum at forty years just as C.C. had said. My heart sank extremely low. Twelve years was a lifetime to me literally. I was only eighteen and to be locked up until I was thirty years old was unimaginable. My mind raced as I realized that twelve years, as far as schooling went, was my whole life. I became sick and the next morning did not even eat breakfast.

As days went by, I found myself reading more and more of the Bible starting from the beginning. I always knew that God had a purpose for my life and that knowledge was made most clear to me at Pastor Bill's church. I had never felt more close to God than when I attended his church, and I wanted to have that feeling again. I wanted to have the knowledge of the entire Bible because I felt so strongly at the time that no one else could get me through this time in my life.

I wrote my mother and sister three weeks into my stay at the Portage County Jail and about and a half in, I received a visit from Cameron, my sister, and my mother. I told them the seriousness of my case and that I probably needed a good lawyer. C.C. told me that if I did not get a paid lawyer that I would be "scratched," meaning that I would get a lot of time. The visit ended with a prayer and before my sister and Cameron left, I was given the news that my seventeen-year-old sister was pregnant to due in June. Her boyfriend since she was fifteen, Thomas was the father and just like me happened to be locked up at the time. I went back to the block at the time, and, like I did every day and night, I prayed in hopes that I could get around this mess.

Two months in, I was given my first pre-trial. This is where your lawyer talks to the prosecutor to try to get the best deal for you as far as time. "Don't take the first deal they give you, hold out for a while." C.C. said the morning before I left. I was told that Van was in the jail, but I had yet to see him and felt a lot of anger toward him for "snitching on me." I was escorted to court on a court bus with about seven other inmates, male and female. When we got to court we were all huddled onto an elevator and put in a holding cell. The guys in one, the girls in the other. I waited in the holding area for over an hour until I was called upstairs to the courtroom. In the courtroom I was seated in a chair surrounded by other chairs where the Jury box would be in a trial. A man came to greet me. "My name is Mr. Emilio, your Public Defender" the man said. While my Public Defender walked away to talk to the Prosecutor, I sat to wait for what I thought would be a good deal. I had never been in any trouble as an adult and nothing really outstanding as a Juvenile aside from probation and a few days in the Detention Center. My Lawyer came back and told me that he would try to get this dropped to a couple of Felony 3 charges, which held a maximum 5 years a piece, and at minimum, 1 year each. As he walked away again, I sat and talked to a couple of the guys around me and conversed about what they were facing. Most of them facing no more than 5 years maximum and one facing ten. I was facing forty. My lawyer came back with a face that said "I tried." He told me that they wanted to keep the Felonies at 1st Degree, but would drop them to two felonies of the 1st degree, and would give me a deal of six years. Six years was outrageous to me and just as C.C. told me, I turned down the first deal. Six years was a long way from 40 years, a very long way, but I had never served more than a few days in jail. Six years was unimaginable. I would miss so much of my life. I would only be 24 when I got out, but at that time it felt like a lifetime. On the way back, on the court bus, one of the girls spoke to me. "Your name is Cedric isn't it?" "Yeah" I replied. "I think I seen your case in the paper" she said. Her name was Ristina and she told me she was also in jail for robbery charges. We said our good-byes and I told her that we would probably see each other again on the court bus. I walked back to my block to find the scenery the same as it always was. C.C. was in his law book, most of the rest of the block win their cell or playing cards and I went to lay down. As I lie down I thought many thoughts. Most of them being hurting Van when I see him simply because he was the main reason I was in here. "How did he even get caught?" I thought aloud. I prayed and went to sleep, hoping that this was all a dream.

The next morning after breakfast my name was called. "Harden, pack it up, you're going to General Population." There were talks about general population while I was in the maximum security block. People said it made the time go quicker and it was more freedom. I packed up my things and walked down the hall to DM5 which was one of the two population pods. When

I walked inside there were about 50 people walking around the pod that was filled with circular tables and chairs. Instead of one shower like "Max," Population called "GP" had four showers, four phones, an officer working inside the actual block, and to my surprise a washer and dryer. In Max we gave our clothes to the block porter and he washed them. I put my things in my cell and walked around to get a feel of the block.

Most of the guys in the block walked in circles around the block and so I followed suit. "Ced, wats up?" A guy yelled out. I looked around to see it was a guy that was in Max with me named Ryan. An older war vet who did heroin and was out of his mind. He loved playing cards and arguing with people. He was also a surprisingly good basketball player, almost unreal for his height and build. I talked to Ryan for a while before I went into my cell which was much different than in Max, because Now I could open it with my hand and the button I used to get my door slid open in Max was the button used for notifying the C.O. to unlock your door in population. GP was more comfortable and it did make me more cautious at the same time. I didn't like being around so many people at one time, especially since, even though I had been incarcerated for two months, I was new to jail and still expected it to be like the movies. Population was fun at times, for jail. At least more than Max. In Max if you went to play basketball in the gym you were probably by yourself, but in G.P. you would go and play with a group of guys. A trio from Cleveland named Al, Sam, and Ric were the guys I hung out with. Sam was big guy at about six feet, 7, 300 pounds, pure muscle; he was one of the guys you would expect to see in a jail movie. I ate with them at lunch as we both told different stories about Cleveland. I was nineteen, they were Rick, twenty-six; Al, twenty-seven; and Sam, twenty-eight, which made them kind of like big brothers to me. All of them had a prison number. Rick had a juvenile prison number. They were serving six months for credit card fraud which was now chunk change to me, considering I already had three months in. I stayed in the church heavily and every time there was a service I attended it. I read my Bible all the time during lockdowns and wrote in a notebook the scriptures that I liked and felt related to my circumstances. I was always going to court. DD let me have one of his law books and I stayed in it just as much as I did the Bible. Every time I went to court, I tried my hardest to convince my public defender that I had no weapon and that the weapons did not belong to me which made the charge a felony two or three, but the prosecutor wouldn't budge. They wanted to make an example out of me. Kent State was a good school, and I messed up its reputation by robbing people on campus. They wanted six years out of me, and every time I went to court, that was the offer. About four and a half months into my sentence, I started to get extremely homesick. I tried to call bondsmen. I asked my mother to put up her house. I wanted to leave here bad. But it was all to no avail. I was stuck with a $500,000 bond and I wasn't going anywhere. After Ric, Al, and Sam went home, I got a new cellmate named Hosea. Hosea was from Honduras. He was as black as any black person I had ever seen, but he spoke Spanish. Hosea had an almost identical case to mine. He had committed a robbery on campus, but he was actually enrolled at Kent during the time. He also had two codefendants, who both told on him. He, however, had no weapons, but did assault somebody and fractured their jawbone.

Hosea and I bonded heavily because of our similarities. I was only a month older than him and just like me, he had celebrated his birthday in jail. As I grew stronger in my faith, Hosea did too. He started to attend church with me as well as read our bibles during lock down times. I was so heavy in the word, I had pages upon pages of scriptures and would read them with Hosea to help him understand them. I felt the Holy Spirit in me. I thirsted for God because of my situation. I wanted to find a way out. "His strength is made perfect in our weakness," says the Bible, and I had never been weaker. Hosea and I played dominoes together and worked out all the time. He was a good friend. He was facing a felony of the second degree, and I always comforted him in letting him know that he was much better off than me. All of Hosea's codefendants had told on him, and so did mine, or at least the ones they could find. Don was still out there living his life, thanks to me, and because of my "Hood morals. Snitches get stitches," I couldn't say a word. Hosea and I were given our discovery motions by our lawyers which showed all the evidence the state had against us. The shock I felt looking through it was memorable to say the least. They had so much, but nothing at all. What surprised me were the people they brought into the case.

They had talked to Nikki who identified that it was me with Van in the store, and they even talked with Diore who snitched me out by telling them I was a gangster disciple, and that I sold weed on campus. It was unreal and I felt my cell getting a little smaller day by day.

Section 17

Darkest Days (God is talking and I hear him now)

I began to have dreams that were not understandable, but because of the spirit of God in me, I knew that they had meaning. One dream I had was one where my mother was in jail with me, going to a church service. I asked her why she was in jail, and she told me that she had stolen some furniture. I didn't understand why my mother would steal furniture, moreover, I couldn't understand why she didn't bond herself out of what was only a $1000 bond. In the dream, a guy asked who she was and instead of telling him, I reached to pull a picture of me and my sister out of my mom's purse (which she ironically had) and when I did, my mom slapped my hand and told me don't do that as if she was ashamed for anyone to know I was her son. I began to have many more dreams and because of prayer and fasting, I was able to interpret them. I started to send my mother my dreams and interpretations, which blew her mind.

Five months into my stay at Portage County Jail, I saw Van for the first time. Amazingly, he was in the block directly across from me, DM6. He looked terrified to see me, and of course he would. Guys in the block knew about my case so well, people yelled out, "There goes your "codefendant right there." "Get him." I really wanted to, but the spirit of God that resided in me filled me with shame at the thought of hurting this man.

When the realization kicked in, that I was not going to be going anywhere, anytime soon, I started to play poker. Poker was common, and was played every day and after a week or two of playing, I couldn't lose. We only played for envelopes. I would win twenty envelopes or better. Some days, I would win thirty or more. I had so many that I would sell them for food. I thanked God for my winnings in the poker. Poker definitely made the clock tick. Days would go by as soon as they started.

When Hosea went back to court for his final trial, he was sentenced to five years. He came back with a look of great sadness and it was a while before we could sit down and talk. When we got to the cell he said, "My mom fainted in the courtroom." Five years was a lot of time for a college kid who never did a day in jail, but Hosea was only nineteen and would still have a full life ahead of him when he got out. The night Hosea was sentenced, we sat in silence. I knew that I would have to serve as much or more even though I wanted to believe that I could beat this case.

When I went back to court for the tenth time, once again, I refused the six years. My public defender was new, and he told me that they now found Don. My heart sank. I still felt like he would stay solid. A few days after the pretrial, my lawyer came to see me and showed me the statements from Don showing that he too had told on me. "This is the last day to accept the offer," my lawyer said. "If not, we are going to trial, and there is no possible way we can win, and you will get double digit time." Once again, I refused the deal and a week after I was brought into court. Surprisingly, my father and sister were at this court hearing.

My lawyer walked over to me and said, "They feel like they have a stronger case, and are now giving you one final deal of eight years before they take it to trial. I'm going to give you a second to talk this over with your family."

My father and sister came over to me crying. My mother could not bear to be there. "Please take this deal, if you don't, you will never get out." Their sadness barely fazed me, but because of love, I gave in and agreed to take the deal. The following week, I was shipped off to Lorain Correction Institution. I had served ten months in the county altogether and had no idea what awaited me in prison. Hopefully, I could continue in my walk with God because it truly felt like he was all I had to rely on…

A note to my son,

As you enter into the walls of prison, I want you to know that I love you and my prayers are with you. The word of God is all you have now. Remember these verses:

Psalm 33:18King James Version (KJV)

18 Behold, the eye of the Lord is upon them that fear him, upon them that hope in his mercy

Proverbs 3:1-621st Century King James Version (KJ21)

3 My son, forget not my law, but let thine heart keep my commandments;

2 for length of days and long life and peace shall they add to thee.

3 Let not mercy and truth forsake thee; bind them about thy neck, write them upon the tablet of thine heart.

4 So shalt thou find favor and good understanding in the sight of God and man.

5 Trust in the Lord with all thine heart, and lean not unto thine own understanding;

6 in all thy ways acknowledge Him, and He shall direct thy paths.

To be continued.

About the Author

Servant Claudia M. Bolden Harden is a native of Cleveland. She earned her Bachelor of Science, Master of Education and Education Specialist degrees from Kent State University.

After serving in education for 30 years as a teacher, counselor and principal of her high school (Shaw High School, East Cleveland, Ohio); she was compelled to resign and retire to pursue her dream of empowering others to change their perspective about life through praise and prayer. Claudia is a licensed minister, Teacher, Spiritual Leader, Pastoral Counselor and Consultant.

Claudia is passionate and serious about serving God. She is launching a Clarion call for prayer. She is committed to serving God through prayer, praise, writing, speaking, and teaching. She is so grateful to God for using her as a Vessel to pour into the lives of others.

She has collaborated with her son, Cedric Harden to write their first book entitled Chained 2 Change, her son's story.

Her mantra:

We must pray
Prayer is not an option
Imagine the blessings

"Train up a child in the way he should go and when he's old, he will not depart from it." Proverbs 22:6

CPSIA information can be obtained
at www.ICGtesting.com
Printed in the USA
FFOW01n2044220915
17013FF

9 781681 390307